Ten Fami[] []s

on Dar~~~~~~~

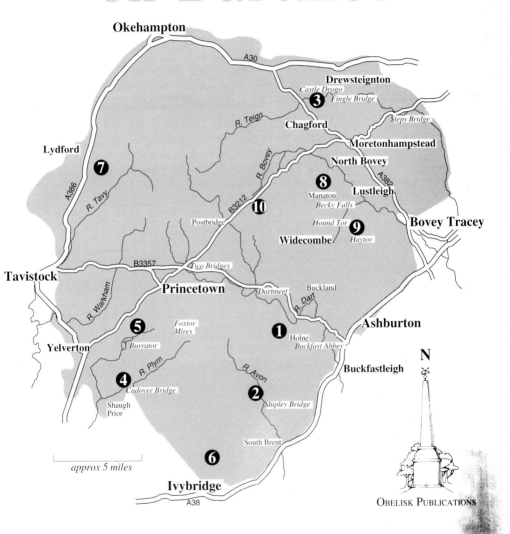

Okehampton

A30

Drewsteignton
Castle Drogo
❸ *Fingle Bridge*

R. Teign
Chagford
Steps Bridge

Lydford
Moretonhampstead
North Bovey
❼
R. Bovey
A382
❽
R. Tavy
A386
Manaton   Lustleigh
B3212   ❿
Becky Falls
Postbridge   *Hound Tor* ❾   Bovey Tracey
Widecombe   *Haytor*

B3357   *Two Bridges*
Tavistock
R. Walkham
Princetown   *Dartmeet*   Buckland
R. Dart
Ashburton
❺   *Foxtor Mires*   ❶
Yelverton   *Burrator*   *Holne*
Buckfast Abbey
R. Plym   *R. Avon*   Buckfastleigh   N
❹
Cadover Bridge
Shaugh Prior   ❷   *Shipley Bridge*

South Brent

approx 5 miles   ❻

Ivybridge
A38   OBELISK PUBLICATIONS

Sally & Chips Barber
(with Andrea, Jenna and Jimmy!)

ALSO BY THE AUTHORS
Dark and Dastardly Dartmoor • Weird and Wonderful Dartmoor
Ghastly and Ghostly Devon • Haunted Pubs in Devon
Six Short Pub Walks on Dartmoor • Walks on and around Woodbury Common
Ten Family Walks in East Devon • Short Circular Walks in and around Sidmouth
Diary of a Dartmoor Walker • Diary of a Devonshire Walker
The Great Little Dartmoor Book • The Great Little Chagford Book
The Teign Valley of Yesteryear I and II
Princetown of Yesteryear I and II
Made in Devon *(with David FitzGerald)* • The Dartmoor Quiz Book
Colourful Dartmoor • The Dartmoor Quiz Book
Cranmere Pool – The First Dartmoor Letterbox
Widecombe – A Visitor's Guide • Railways on and around Dartmoor
Around and About Tavistock • Along the Tavy
Around and About Roborough Down • Around and About Lustleigh

OTHER 'WALKING' OR 'DARTMOOR' TITLES FROM OBELISK PUBLICATIONS INCLUDE:
The Great Walks of Dartmoor, *Terry Bound*
The A to Z of Dartmoor Tors, *Terry Bound*
Walks in the Chagford Countryside, *Terry Bound*
Under Sail through South Devon & Dartmoor, *Raymond B. Cattell*
The Templer Way, *Derek Beavis*
Walks in the South Hams, *Brian Carter*
Pub Walks in the Haldon Hills, *Brian Carter*
Walks in the Totnes Countryside, *Bob Mann*
Walks in the Shadow of Dartmoor, *Denis McCallum*
Walks in Tamar and Tavy Country, *Denis McCallum*
The Dartmoor Mountain Bike Guide, *Peter Barnes*
Circular Walks on Eastern Dartmoor, *Liz Jones*
Nine Short Pub Walks in and around Torbay, *Brian Carter*
Dartmoor Letterboxing – A Guide for Beginners, *Kevin Weall*

**We have over 160 Devon titles – for a current list please write to Obelisk Publications,
2 Church Hill, Pinhoe, Exeter, EX4 9ER or telephone (01392) 468556**

PLATE ACKNOWLEDGEMENTS
All sketch maps drawn from an out-of-copyright source by Sally Barber
All photographs by or belonging to Chips Barber

*First published in 1990 (0 946651 41 8), Reprinted in 1992 and 1993
Revised edition (0 946651 99 X) published in 1994
Reprinted in 1995, 1997, 1999 and 2000 by
Obelisk Publications, 2 Church Hill, Pinhoe, Exeter, Devon
Designed by Chips and Sally Barber
Printed in Great Britain*

© Sally & Chips Barber

INTRODUCTION

Dartmoor has one square mile for each day of the year – 365 to save you working it out! This sounds like a vast expanse with plenty to chose from for a short walk with the family. However, some of these many square miles are on private land, many are under great coniferous forests whilst others are extensive tracts of monotonous mires. This little book will help you find those square miles where you can wander to your heart's content, safe in the knowledge that you will eventually return to your vehicle and not get lost in this lovely landscape.

Ten Family Walks on Dartmoor is designed to offer you a variety of walks and, providing you encounter reasonable weather conditions, these walks should take you through some memorable countryside. The bulk of the walks follow tracks and try to avoid tedious road walking. The sketch maps with each walk are designed to provide you with a rough guide but it is highly recommended that you invest either in a copy of the Dartmoor Tourist Map, which gives detail at a scale of one inch to a mile, or, if you prefer far more detail, the Outdoor Leisure, number 28, is excellent value. (Both are extremely large maps and they are better folded to the portion you need as many a copy has been whisked away by a spirited Dartmoor gale! Also, being made of paper they tear easily so a map case is recommended.)

Although fairly confident that the route instructions are adequate, as time passes things change, plus of course some folk will inevitably interpret details in a different way to that intended – so good planning is the key! Read the walks through before you do them, compare the sketch map route with your map and note, in advance, the sort of experience you are likely to encounter. Remember to keep an eye on the weather and be prepared to dress for the conditions. (Some people take off wearing such things as sandals or flip flops!) These Dartmoor walks, however easy, still merit strong, sensible footwear, a good waterproof and, bearing in mind that you may be out for a few hours, take something to eat and drink just in case your energy level drains and needs to be recharged.

Hopefully you haven't been put off but "forewarned is forearmed" and if you are fully prepared for all eventualities, you will probably sail around the routes wondering what all the fuss was about! There are some wonderful walks awaiting you and we are sure the extremely modest outlay for this publication will be more than repaid after trying just a few of them!

You will notice references to our other titles throughout the text. The reasons for this are twofold: firstly it would be impossible, in such a small book, to include all the relevant facts and interesting snippets of information where they occur on each walk; and secondly – you might just be tempted enough to go out and buy a copy for yourself! The books referred to are: *Diary of a Dartmoor Walker* and *Diary of a Devonshire Walker* (lively accounts of mishaps and misdeeds on longish walks all over Dartmoor and Devon – which you may or may not like to attempt to follow yourself); *Dark and Dastardly Dartmoor* (all the Dartmoor legends and ghostly tales); *Made in Devon* (a fascinating look at some of the many television programmes, commercials and feature films which have been made wholly or partly in Devon); and *The Great Little Dartmoor Book* (all about Dartmoor's beauty spots, industry, popular villages and towns, wildlife, pubs, letterboxes etc, beautifully illustrated with pen and ink line drawings).

❶ A Hike Around Holne Moor

The beautiful moorland parish of Holne contains some of the finest scenery in Devon, a mixture of open moorland punctuated by deep wooded combes, some filled with quiet babbling brooks, others with strong torrents.

The starting point for this lovely little three mile romp is a car park in a disused quarry (SX 699 697). To reach this point, which is about half a mile to the north west of Holne, it will be easiest to get to from the A38 at Ashburton. The B3357 leaves the south west side of town so take this meandering road which leads over the lovely Holne Bridge and follow the signs towards Holne Village. As you approach Holne you will find that the road towards the moor doesn't actually pass through the village centre but veers to its right and starts to climb towards the open moor. The starting point is immediately on your left hand side just beyond the cattle grid. There is enough room for about 8 – 10 cars.

If you arrive from the Hexworthy direction the disused quarry will be on your right immediately above the cattle grid. The nearest public toilets are a mile away at Venford Reservoir.

Come out of the car park entrance and turn right onto the track that leads towards 'Stone Shallows' which is shown as 'The Shanty' on the 1:25 000 map. Do not enter this private property but on reaching it head right and follow the edge of it for a short distance. At the end of the wall the track climbs slightly more steeply. The track has a kink and in about 20 yards you should fork off to the right.

A small stream is soon encountered but is easily negotiated. You are heading for the top of the highest enclosed field that you can see ahead of you. Don't worry – the terrain is easy on the foot and the track climbs a gentle gradient all the way up.

On reaching the top of this field the track gives way to being more of a path so follow it along the stone wall. If you have not stopped to survey the view, then perhaps you had better do so now. You are on the high edge of the open rolling southern moor. To the south east the land falls away dramatically to create a tremendous view of a large part of eastern Dartmoor and a vast area of South Devon. From some angles you will be able to spy Buckfast Abbey through a gap in the hills that are near it. Beyond lies the beautiful countryside

N

approx half a mile

To Venford Reservoir

P

Stone Shallows

Wheat Emma Leat

The Sandy Way

Greatcombe

Michelcombe

Holne

To Ashburton

To Buckfast

Scorriton

that fringes the great tourist area of Torbay. The only thing that this part of the moor lacks is the typical tor scenery, normally such a distinctive feature of most Dartmoor landscapes. Still if it's one of those diamond days that can occur you won't mind too much. The wall on the left ends and you will see lower down the hillside a dry watercourse contouring the hill, which is the Wheal Emma Leat, ideal for non swimmers. It is one of many on Dartmoor that provided a source of power for machinery. 'Wheal' is an old Celtic word that means mine so quote this gem of industrial archaeological knowledge to your companions and then perhaps you too might be regarded as a 'mine' of information!

Avoid the temptation to go straight down the hill. It is easier to contour the hillside for a bit and gradually drop down to the leat.

The Wheal Emma Leat was cut in 1859 and ran all the way from the Swincombe River, a tributary of the West Dart, around the hills for some nine miles to bring extra water to the River Mardle. The latter was the source of water power to a number of mining operations, which included the Wheal Emma copper mine, hence the leat's name, near Buckfastleigh. This mine joined forces with the nearby Brockwood Mine to form a company called South Devon United (not to be mistaken for a soccer team)! The Golden Age for this undertaking was between 1861–77 when many thousands of tons of copper were raised. The workings, in the valleys below, went over 700 feet below ground. Two small footbridges cross it but today they remain redundant. If you walk along the bed of the former leat take care to look up occasionally as a small tree grows in the centre of it at one point. You are not going to follow it too far but when you do, stay with it until you reach a point where a track comes down the hill to cross it where six slabs of granite act as a bridge over the leat. There are other tracks and other little bridges but this is the one you require. Turn left and go downhill along the path, which is known as the Sandy Way. You will see that it is signposted to Michelcombe. Follow it.

The Sandy Way is an ancient path which, in early times, was probably used as a major trackway between Ashburton (where they all speaks prapper Deb'n) and Tavistock. The lane, most likely an old cattle droving route, descends for about half a mile to reach the hamlet of Michelcombe (locals often call it "Mutchecum"). Although it is a stony thoroughfare it remains a pleasant corridor, passing between fields where sheep seem to predominate. If passing at dusk, listen carefully – you may hear them counting people in an attempt to get to sleep!

Almost at the bottom of this hill, a signposted track off to the left should be taken, which immediately passes an attractive cottage to cross a stream supplemented by water from the Holne Moor Leat. Alas, what has gone down must needs now go up! To regain the dizzy heights of Holne Moor this track must be followed. Although the way is steep, long and arduous, the many twists and turns in the track and the path make it an enjoyable climb.

At the end of the path there are no indicators to point the way. If you ascend the hill you will see the extensive rooftops of 'The Shanty' to your right. If you keep this to your right and head back over the moor you should have no difficulty in relocating the quarry. The view now lies across the Double Dart, over Holne Chase and beyond to such eminences as Buckland Beacon.

In recommendation, our children enjoyed this particular walk immensely and we think it is one of the best on the moor!

❷   A Saunter at Shipley Bridge

Shipley Bridge is one of the loveliest locations in Devon and inevitably it is a popular place. It lies on the River Avon about two miles to the north-north-west of South Brent. Although it can be approached from South Brent the lane is tortuous, and motorists who are unfamiliar with the twists and turns of the road, might prefer to reach the destination with the signposted road that leads from the Marley Head junction on the A38. This climbs over the shoulder of the distinct Brent Hill and is a slightly less nerve-racking way to get to Shipley Bridge (Avon Dam). Unfortunately, on fine days parking can be a problem as all the world and a few more seem determined to find a suitable niche for their vehicle right here. Don't be put off though because this walk has much to commend it.

We should start with a cautionary word. Although there are toilets at Shipley, they tend to be seasonal so if you are not the adventurous sort, who enjoys communing with nature, bear in mind that you will be gone for a few hours!

The road from Shipley Bridge up to the Avon Dam

The first section of this walk is ideal for those who have youngsters in prams, or people in wheelchairs. A well-surfaced road leads up the valley from Shipley Bridge to the Avon Dam. It is a gentle gradient upwards, demanding very little exertion on the up journey, which follows that the return journey down the valley is even simpler! It is about one and a half miles up to the dam and, of course, the same back. For the benefit of this account to be more historically interesting, however, the route has been extended to create an overall walk at just about five miles. The extended 'bit' will certainly enable participants to sample a more solitary section of the moor.

The remains of buildings, which form the western margin of the car park, are the former clay dries where clays brought down a few miles from Bala Brook Head were processed. In a short distance you will see a largish rock beside the road on the left hand side. This is the Hunters' Stone. On it you may be able to identify the names of celebrated local huntsmen who once rode these moors. On the right side of the path the River Avon can be seen tumbling steeply downwards in a perpetual rush to reach the sea in Bigbury Bay. Its local name is the Aune and the map proudly proclaims the point where it rises as Aune Head, a remote, wild and wet location.

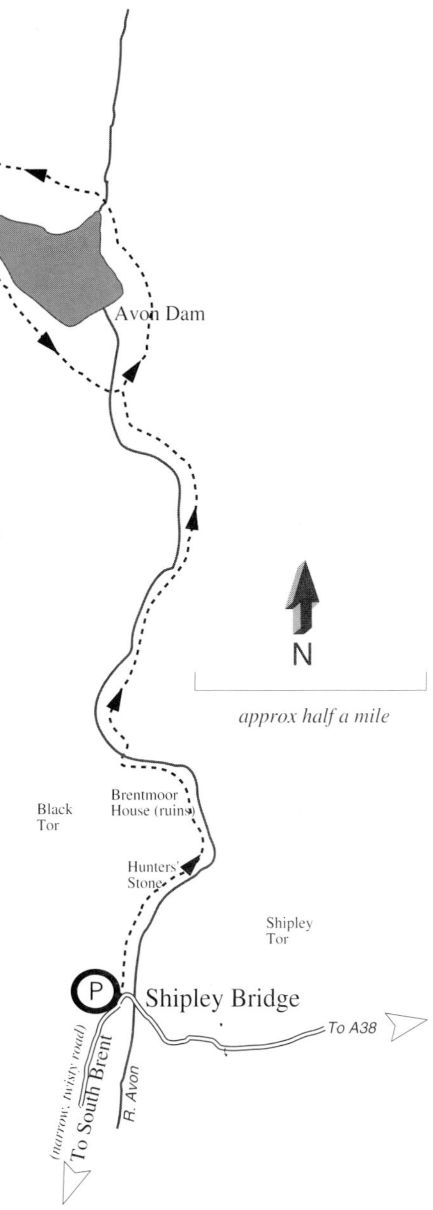

A gateway with stone pillars is soon reached but more noticeable is the jungle of rhododendrons, which choke this next section of the walk. The gateway was the entrance to Brentmoor House, once a substantial moorland residence and for several years, prior to its demolition in 1968, a youth hostel. In its grounds, close to the side of the hill and amidst the rhododendrons, you may care to leave the track to seek out a memorial to a little girl who died here. More information is given in *Diary of a Devonshire Walker*.

Above this former house the road crosses the Avon and follows the east bank northwards. Should there be a keen prevailing westerly wind blowing you will appreciate the sheltered nature of this valley. However if it's a northerly breeze or, even worse, from the north-east you may curse the way it can funnel the wind to such an extent that it is a formidable struggle to make progress up the valley – conversely it is hard to restrain yourself from running back down it on your return! The trough-like nature of this section of the valley has earned it the name 'Long-a-Traw'.

Ahead lies the Avon Dam, an impressive structure designed to store water for people in the Totnes and South Hams areas. In the lee of the dam there is often shelter on inclement days. It you find yourself speculating as to what it might be like if the dam

Map labels: R. Avon · Avon Dam · N · approx half a mile · Black Tor · Brentmoor House (ruins) · Hunters' Stone · Shipley Tor · Shipley Bridge · To A38 · (narrow, twisty road) To South Brent · R. Avon · P

The Avon Dam

suddenly burst, you can be reassured that this is a geologically stable region and the dam has stood there quite unperturbed since the mid 1950s.

In severe drought years when the level of the reservoir drops, an ancient settlement is revealed on the north-east side of the lake close to where the Brockhill streams enters it. It is curious to note that at such times many hundreds of visitors make a pilgrimage to see something which isn't there, i.e. the lack of water.

If your legs have almost had enough it is quite acceptable to turn around to stroll leisurely back to your car at Shipley Bridge. Should you require more brisk exercise, however, you can do a lap of honour of the lake. On the north-east side of the reservoir you will pick up a well-defined track called the Abbots' Way, an ancient routeway linking abbeys on opposing sides of Dartmoor (see *Diary of a Dartmoor Walker*). About 500 yards above the top of the lake it will lead you to a crossing point over the Avon, close to where the Western Wella Brook arrives from the north. The route back to the dam lies along the steeper sloping western bank of the reservoir. The route back to Shipley is all downhill stuff and, if the season is right, the ice cream van will look extremely inviting!

❸　A Trek Around the Teign

Drewsteignton is a small hilltop village on the edge of the Dartmoor National Park. The surrounding scenery is not that of open moorland country but has always proved popular with walkers as it is beautiful. There are many granite-built cottages in the square and the attractive Holy Trinity Church completes the rural scene. Here is the starting place for a circular walk of about four to five miles.

Although there are a few short, sharp ascents you start by leaving the square on the road towards Chagford. Almost immediately opposite the former village school, an obvious track leads off to the left. This is a section of the famous 'Two Moors Way' route which spans both Dartmoor and Exmoor, and the many miles of farmland in between.

At first you'll be led into a false sense of security as the path carries you downwards into the valley of the small tributary stream that runs down to Fingle Bridge. Beyond the stream is a steepish climb where it is better to conserve the air in your lungs for scaling the hill rather than exchanging words with your companions on the

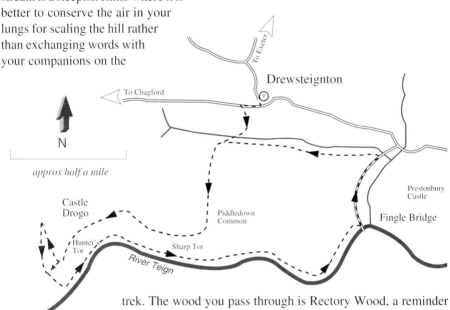

trek. The wood you pass through is Rectory Wood, a reminder that once the church owned great areas of lands – these are called Glebelands. The hill begins to level out and a gentle drop brings you out to the much walked Hunters' Path, high above the valley of the Teign. To your left or east is Drewston Common but to your right/west is Piddledown Common, an emotive name which conjures up visions of Devon's (at times) inclement weather.

On reaching a T-junction of paths you should head west or right and soon you will reach the most impressive rocky outcrop known as Sharp Tor. It is not like typical Dartmoor tors but juts out spectacularly from the side of the gorge. It is a good vantage point over the wooded valley way below, Castle Drogo is away to your right and, in the distance, you might be able to pick out the higher northern moors of Dartmoor – Hangingstone Hill, Kestor Rock and Fernworthy Forest. These are just some of the landmarks you may identify whilst taking a well-earned breather. The one minor drawback of the Teign Gorge

The view from the Hunters' Path looking towards Sharp Tor many years ago. The Fisherman's Path, now hidden by trees, can be seen.

The River Teign

is that on hot, sunny days, great armies of red ants will be seen scurrying about – so be warned and carefully choose your site for refreshments!

The track is easy to follow as it contours the hillside. This part of the moor appears in almost every walking book and as a consequence the track, which was only a footstep wide some thirty years ago, is now quite broad. Still it offers an opportunity to say 'hello' to walkers heading in the opposite direction so be prepared to be sociable as you head on below Castle Drogo to reach a low spur where the path veers sharply away from the main valley.

You now have a choice, which will depend on your state of mind and/or your ability to cope with steep downward gradients. You may either opt for the short, sharp, steep, short-cut down to the bottom of the hill (and one slip will ensure that it *will* be short and sharp so great care should be taken) or you may prefer the more dignified, laid-back route which follows the track to the north for about 400 yards before almost doubling back on itself to reach the same point at Coombe. It is your day out so you will know better what suits your needs. Head down to the river, which is wider and more distinct than the stream flowing into it.

The path you now follow is the Fisherman's Path, which is a logical title considering that this is a fine river for fishing. The National Trust have done a good job in making this path, along the north bank of the river, an easier and safer thoroughfare. There are a few minor climbs on the first section but soon the path becomes a tame affair and the two miles to Fingle Bridge will simply help to create an appetite and a thirst. If this walk is done in high summer, the woods will seem like a dense verdant jungle, whereas in autumn it is a golden paradise – nowhere are the changing seasons so obvious.

Fingle Bridge straddles the river at a point where a tributary stream, which rises near Whiddon Down on the A30, cuts a steep entry down to this beauty

The Fisherman's Path

spot. The stream has cut a gap between Prestonbury Castle, an Iron Age Hill Fort, and Drewston Common. The road builders have taken advantage of this deep cleft in the hills to forge a route to Fingle. On fine days it is a very popular spot. Several TV commercials have been filmed here for products as diverse as gas, yogurt and an airline company (for full details of these and other films and TV features filmed in the county you should read *Made in Devon*).

The Angler's Rest grew from the humble beginnings of a tea shelter at the turn of the century into the fine building you see today. Should you need light refreshment or a full

The old Tea Shelter at Fingle Bridge

blown meal you can satisfy your desires here.

A few hours will probably have elapsed since you set out so, to complete this stroll, follow the road out of Fingle towards Drewsteignton and, after about 500 yards, turn left into the path which will take you along the northern limit of Rectory Wood. In about half a mile you will recognise where you were earlier in the day. Follow the track up and right back to Drewsteignton.

Although deer are extremely rare on the open moorlands of Dartmoor they are in fact common in the woods along the Teign Gorge. The quieter you are and the closer you are to the extremes of the day – early morning/late evening – will govern your chances of spotting them. As you will have spent much of the walk espying Castle Drogo (see *The Great Little Dartmoor Book*) it might be an idea to incorporate a visit with your day out. Many Dartmoor walking enthusiasts use this area as a standby area when they simply have to get out for a walk and the weather conditions

Fingle Bridge

on the open moor are too wild and woolly. Invariably the sheltered nature of the Teign Valley provides the perfect alternative.

❹ A Perfect Plym Perambulation

Cadover Bridge could be called Dartmoor-on-Sea because, on fine days, many hundreds of people, mainly Plymothians, congregate here *en masse* to enjoy this popular beauty spot. Situated on the River Plym, it is a jewel set in a landscape pitted with enormous china clay quarries – a vitally important raw material for so many industries. Its location on the south western corner of Dartmoor, not too many miles from Plymouth, is the key to its popularity and it is well signposted from most directions. However, before you declare that you want to walk on Dartmoor to get *away* from the masses, not to join them, be assured that on leaving the car park you will soon be able to enjoy a lovely, almost spectacular, mixed four mile walk of woodland and open moor in virtual solitude. But you will have to keep an eye out for the Devil – he is said to live along this route!

Park in the large car park on the south bank of the Plym just below the bridge. If you have arrived before the ice cream van

To Yelverton

Wigford Down

River Meavy

Cadover Cross

Cadover Bridge

P

Dewerstone

The Pipe Track

To Plymouth

River Plym

Shaugh Bridge

N

approx half a mile

Shaugh Prior

To Plympton and Ivybridge

you will have nothing to distract you from heading in the opposite direction to the bridge, climbing the stile and heading south westwards away from Cadover.

The first part of the walk is generally easy and for the main part follows the Pipe Track. This is aptly named as it follows the line of a pipe that carried china clay in suspension (water) down to the drying kilns at Shaugh Bridge, where you will be later.

The path is pleasant and how much water you will see or hear in the Plym, deep in the valley below, will depend on the season. North Wood can seem almost jungle-like in high summer but very stark in the depths of winter. In between times are probably the best, when spring is in the air or autumn endows this valley with a golden cloak.

North Wood is soon left behind as the track contours the side of West Down. On the opposite side of the valley can be seen the great crags of the Dewerstone. 'Dewer' is one of many words used by Devonshire folk for the Devil, 'Daddy' being another. He is believed to reside in this hillside and legend has it that he casts the souls of unbaptised

The River Plym at Shaugh Bridge

babies over the precipice of this impressive outcrop. This doesn't put climbers off, however, and if your eyesight is good you might well see tiny figures dangling across these rocks. Later you will get to the top of the rocks – by the relatively easy route.

It is now time to apply the brakes as after several hundred yards of gentle downward movement, the track begins to descend far more steeply, with the full force of gravity coming into play. Shaugh Bridge is a beauty spot and it is also an alternative starting/finishing place for this walk. The geographical term for a meeting place of two rivers is a confluence. Here the Plym is joined by its major tributary, the Meavy. Older locals and Dartmoor purists refer to it as the Mewy, a name which has origins in 'Mew' meaning a seagull.

You are at the lowest point of the walk here. In times of heavy rain on the high moors these two watercourses can become raging torrents. The Meavy is less of a threat as its waters are controlled in part by Burrator Reservoir, which lies many miles upstream and was opened in 1898 to supply Plymouth. The Plym has removed various bridges in times of anger but, hopefully, the latest foot bridge spanning the Plym will be in tact. You only have to cross one river in order to reach the spur between the Plym and the Meavy so – Do not cross Shaugh Bridge!

Your flirtation with these two rivers is brief for the path you follow is along neither. Instead you take the rough and rocky way, in the first instance, to a sharp bend to the left. Your possible breathlessness will be greatly relieved as the track levels out to pass a disused quarry before heading on to the right. The track was once a former horse-drawn railway and the observant wayfarer will detect evidence of this inclined plane, if one is so inclined! Whether you have leanings towards an interest in industrial archaeology or not doesn't matter too much for your next half mile is upwards! After a long, straightish upward section the track doubles back on itself and, as you approach the summit, becomes far more of a normal type of path.

As promised earlier, now is your chance to visit the rocks on the edge of the Dewerstone, partly for a well-earned rest and partly to survey your environs from this high rocky pinnacle .

The rest of the walk is comparatively easy, almost an anticlimax. Wigford Down is gentle and you skirt the edge of it heading back towards Cadover Bridge along and above the field enclosures on the right. Leaving the former Iron Age Hill Fort on top of the Dewerstone you have an easy walk of just over three quarters of a mile to the next point of interest, which is the large stone cross near Cadover Bridge. The head of the cross is original but the lower part of its shaft is a replacement – soldiers out on manoeuvres in 1873 found the head of the cross, which they set up, but in 1901 a cow knocked it down, so the new shaft was put in to assure its future. (We didn't discover whether the cow deliberately took a dislike to this landmark or simply wasn't looking where she was going!)

From the cross you should be able to see your vehicle in the car park on the opposite bank and by crossing Cadover Bridge, you will soon reach it.

❺ Beautiful Burrator and Creepy Crazy Well

This splendid little walk through woods, across open moors, past all manner of interesting objects and historical landmarks, is about four and a half miles long. The starting point is the diminutive Norsworthy Bridge (SZ 568 694) a picturesque spot, which straddles the River Meavy or Mewy on the north eastern corner of Burrator Reservoir. There is usually plenty of parking in the vicinity even on a rare, busy day.

Burrator Reservoir

Almost beside Norsworthy Bridge a strong track climbs gently north eastwards. It is your corridor to the moor and should be followed. Almost immediately a tempting wooded path leads away to the left but do not be distracted as your route ascends to the moor to a more open and less peopled environment.

The track is stony and climbs steadily but if you can persuade yourself (and followers) that the effort is worth it, then your rewards will come later and are considerable. Below you on your right will be seen the remains of farm buildings. All the people who farmed in the feeder valleys to Burrator had to leave the watershed for pastures new, although some were allowed to stay on until they passed away. The film *Revolution* (a spectacular flop!) starring Al Pacino and Donald Sutherland, used this area for battle scenes. (For more information read *Made in Devon*.)

By keeping the forest on your left, you will eventually reach a gateway onto the open moor. The track is less demanding on the feet and only needs to be followed for a few hundred yards. As you curve around the first hill you will see a cross silhouetted against the skyline whilst before you, a gully comes down from the left carrying a small watercourse. At this point you should turn left from the track and ascend the hillside above that gully. By doing this you will locate the large water-filled mine workings called Crazy Well, Classonwell or Classiwell Pool.

The legend attached to this pool is discussed in *Dark and Dastardly Dartmoor* but briefly, either a wailing voice calls the name of the next person to die in the Parish of Walkhampton or, on Midsummer's Eve, a reflection of the next victim can be seen. It is also said to be bottomless (the combined lengths of the bell ropes of Walkhampton Church tied together would not reach the bottom, which would make it more than 500 feet deep). However, the likely general depth of the pool is probably about 15 feet but it is possible that there is a shaft in the middle, helping to perpetuate this legend. It is an old tin working and there is evidence all around of this old Dartmoor industry. Another story says that it rises and falls with the tide at Plymouth as it is connected by a massive underground tunnel. The probable reason for developing such tales as these is to put people off from going there and results in the place name of Classiewell (1638) turning into the Crazywell Pool of today. Whatever the state of the tide it is better not to get too near!

If the weather is clear you will see the tip of the mast at North Hessary Tor, the top of which is the highest (man-made) point in the South of England! If you head towards it you will strike the Devonport Leat rattling along towards Raddick Hill. Follow it in the direction that it flows and the next mile or so will take you along quite easily with great views all round.

Burrator is ringed with a number of impressive tors, Leather Tor, Sheeps Tor and Down Tor are the principal peaks. From the lofty heights of the Devonport Leat these can all be spied, the first two rising in stony grandeur, like great rocky cathedrals, from the forest surrounding Burrator Lake.

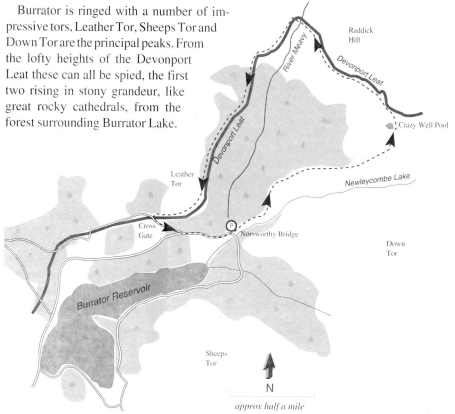

The Devonport Leat wends its way around Raddick Hill before doing a kamikaze act by hurtling steeply and spectacularly down hill. You have to do the same so take care as you descend the hillside. Having done this many times, we recommend the slightly easier Princetown side of the leat as the Burrator side has a few swampy areas. The fleet footed leat follower should not find it too difficult to descend to the iron launder which carries the leat over the River Meavy.

Once across the aqueduct the second half of the walk becomes an easy one. The ground conditions beside the leat affords easy progress and the lovely surroundings can be appreciated without too much distraction.

Perhaps by now you may be a bit inquisitive about this wondrous winding watercourse that you are following. It is many miles long and is fed by the Blackbrook, Cowsic and West Dart rivers. It was opened in 1793 and largely satisfied the needs of Plymouth and Devonport until 1898 when Burrator Reservoir was opened. The Devonport Leat superseded the 17-mile long Drake's Leat, which often dried up in summer and froze up in winter – no small wonder that it was 'deleted'!

The leat enters Stanlake Plantation and the first of two stiles along this section has to be negotiated. A game to occupy the children, who may by now be a little weary, is to get them to estimate how many trout they will spot in the leat during the next mile as far as Cross Gate. Although the trout in the leat are generally small, there are many and on a good day, walking at a gentle pace, it may be possible to see more than a hundred.

Unlike many woodland walks, in predominantly coniferous surroundings, this section has enough twists and turns, open glades and variety of flora to make an extremely interesting romp. In the clearing below the impressive Leather Tor there are fine view across to Sheepstor and down the reservoir towards Meavy.

Stay with the leat along its banks, ignoring all other paths and distractions, until you reach the first cross that appears to have been slightly guillotined. This point is known as Cross Gate and the road, which leads downhill, serves as the way back to the starting point. In a short while the broader road, which circumnavigates the reservoir, will be reached and not long after this your vehicle will be regained. We did this walk before breakfast on a May Day Bank Holiday and didn't see a single person the whole time we were out (or hear a single wail)!

❻ A Hike Around Harford

Harford is a hamlet on the road to nowhere in particular! A narrow country lane (with a generous number of passing places) wends its way high on the hillside above the Erme Valley from Ivybridge, on the southern extremity of Dartmoor. According to signposts, it is only about two and a half miles from Ivybridge to Harford, but it will inevitably seem further due to the twisting nature of this road.

On reaching Harford Church, turn right onto the 'no through road'. This will take you uphill to some gates (which, hopefully, a willing volunteer will leap out of the car to open) at the entrance to a car park which can accommodate about thirty or forty vehicles.

This is a three mile walk, best done on a relatively clear day, mainly so as to enjoy the extensive views, but also to allow you to follow the route instructions more easily. If you have a compass it would be useful as this part of the moor is prone to swift weather changes. The scenery in this part of the Erme Valley is beautiful – a Dartmoor landscape, though lacking in the typical tor type scenery normally found.

From the car park you will need to follow the wall, which you will keep on your left as you head in a general northward direction. When, after a few hundred yards, it starts to bend away from you to head downhill, stop following it. Instead you will need to practice the art of "contouring". This means that instead of going up or down

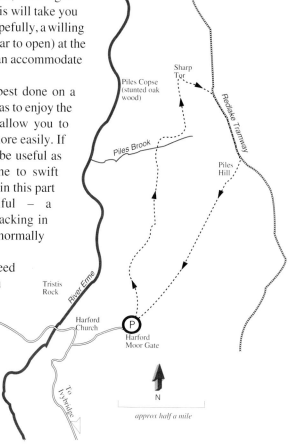

you remain on the same level. It is an easy skill to acquire and results in level walking. The only drawback of contouring is when the hill is so steep that you have to move as if one leg is longer than the other! Fortunately this side of the Erme Valley is not that precipitous and you can proceed ahead for several hundred yards over reasonable ground even when there is no track to follow.

Soon you will see another wall also trying out its contouring skills along the hillside. Follow it, on the moor side, and it will carry you to Piles Gate from where you will begin the steepest climb on the walk up to Sharp Tor.

Sharp Tor is a bit of a misnomer as it is not a sharp landscape feature nor are its rocks jagged. In fact they are ideal for sitting down upon to survey the views it gives over central Southern Dartmoor and of South West Devon. Away to the west you will see the china clay spoil heaps of Lee Moor, and the sprawling urban mass of Plymouth and its Sound are also clearly discernible. You may well appreciate a breather here as it has been a bit of a climb but the rest of the walk is a doddle ...

The River Erme, which flows hundreds of feet below, is regarded as one of the most beautiful in Devon. From here it flows in a generally southward direction for about another twelve miles to reach the sea at Mothecombe, where the opening location shots were filmed for *International Velvet*, starring Tatum O'Neal. (Further details are in *Made in Devon*.)

Just a little to the north west and deep down in the valley is Piles Copse, a wood of stunted pendunculate oak trees, one of three such woods on the moor. The other two are Black Tor Copse, on the West Okement River above Meldon Reservoir, and Wistman's Wood, about three quarters of a mile above Two Bridges on the West Dart River. The latter is a particularly fine example of how such trees survive in the face of adversity – Dartmoor is a wild, wet and windy place so if you have chosen one of its more benign days for this stroll, please appreciate that it does have a fierce climate! The average of 180 rain days a year and the low temperature combine to produce a soil with which only the most stubborn and resistant of trees can cope.

When the climate was marginally warmer and less wet, this part of Dartmoor was particularly favoured by Bronze Age people; there are many pounds, stone rows, stone circles and other remains here as evidence of their previous existence. However, it is a more recent piece of history that will help you on your way. Just a few hundred yards to the east you will see a track, again running along the hillside. Go across to it and then follow it southwards. This is the trackbed of the Redlake Mineral Railway, which was opened in 1911. It ran from the southern tip of the moor at Western Beacon up to Redlake for seven and a half miles. About a hundred workers produced the clay that was carried down this line, a venture which finished, forever, in 1932. The lines were all gone by the end of the following year.

When you reach the trackbed you will also see a line of boundary stones running alongside the line. Follow the railway for about 300 yards. At the end of the straight you will see a slightly elevated slope on your right. This is Piles Hill and is nowhere near as painful as it sounds! To prove to yourself that you are on the right route, you should be able to see the Longstone just a short distance away from the cairn to the south-east.

In order to get back to your vehicle at Harford Moor Gate it will now be necessary to test either your sense of direction or your map skills. The most direct line route back is not all that apparent as you stand on this gently rounded hill of three sides. To get your bearings look to the south west where you will see a small clump of trees on a level down. The down is called Hanger Down so, not surprisingly, the clump is called Hanger Down Clump (it is about 2 miles away). If you make a bee-line for this you will descend the hill, which has some uneven ground, to find your way back.

After a short distance on the descent you will see, just on the other side of the valley, Tristis Rock (also called Hall Tor), which you should keep well to your right. All being well, you should soon complete this relatively easy but immensely enjoyable little walk.

❼ The Tavy Cleave – the Rockiest Valley on Dartmoor!

There is a large car park beside the A386 road between Mary Tavy and Sourton. From the Okehampton direction it is just beyond the cattle grid on your left, where the road enters the open moorland at Willsworthy Down. The reverse applies if you are travelling northwards. The car park is not the nearest point to the area you explore in this outing but access along the surfaced road towards the Tavy Cleave is restricted to army vehicles visiting Willsworthy. Remember to check first that the army are not firing. Should you forget to consult the local press on a preceding Friday, don't hear the local radio announcements or decide not to ring the 'Ansafone' service under 'Army', then you will be able to see if there is firing by spotting a red flag flying on distant White Hill.

This will eventually become a spectacular walk of about four and a half miles, despite starting in decidedly dull surroundings. Follow the road towards the rifle ranges in an easterly direction and uphill. You can walk beside it, which is softer on the feet. There are

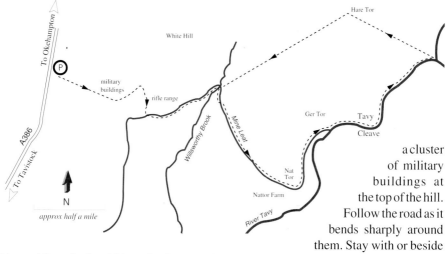

a cluster of military buildings at the top of the hill. Follow the road as it bends sharply around them. Stay with or beside this road for a further 200 yards. On your right hand side is a rough track that goes off at a right angle. It has a low mound beside it, which disappears very quickly. Follow it and in a short distance you will reach a fenced-off rifle range with a gate bearing a large letter 'B'. Skirt the right hand side of the fence and soon you will see a wooden footbridge ahead of you. This is ideal for right-handed walkers who are outward bound and perfect for left-handed walkers who are homeward bound! Precise route descriptions every few yards are no longer necessary once you have crossed the bridge and turned left to follow the leat.

The Reddaford or Mine leat provides an easy way of reaching the Tavy Cleave and, after it turns sharply, good views of the country in around the Tavy Valley will be seen. The small farm on your right is Nattor Farm and as the leat turns to enter the Cleave it passes around the spur containing Nat Tor itself. Most people fail to notice it as they are distracted with the splendid sight that confronts them as they peer up through this spectacular rocky canyon.

Eventually the leat ends at a small intake building, a good spot to take a break beneath the great mass of Ger Tor. The going to this point has been decidedly easy but now a bit more guile and care is needed as the *terra firma* is not so firm as you head toward the most striking part of the Tavy Cleave. It is extremely soft in places, mainly so beside the river as you head eastwards toward a sharp bend.

When the corner is turned a wonderful sight presents itself, a scene which has been heralded as one of the loveliest on the moor by so many great writers. The Tavy drops steeply through this gorge in a succession of miniature rapids and waterfalls whilst on either side steep hillsides rise up like the walls of a great strong castle. A waterfall is soon encountered, a splendid place, and on days when a fierce north westerly breeze blasts the high northern moors, this deep steep valley offers shelter.

No doubt by now the time will have passed by faster than you expected and various alternatives are open to you. The walk can be easily extended to go as far as the confluence with the Rattlebrook to then head over Hare Tor before veering south westwards back to Willsworthy, a total of about six and a quarter miles or, if your family is agile and likes a challenge, the north side of the Tavy Cleave, rising straight up from the waterfall, can be climbed. This is a mixture of clitter (rocky debris strewn on the hillside) and vegetation. This should be taken slowly and is not suitable for very young children. On reaching the summit the most direct way back is over the shoulder of Ger Tor. On a clear day the Mine Leat will be seen from this point and can be easily reached at the point where it sharply turns the corner over the Willsworthy Brook.

Families with young children may wish to retrace their steps because once the leat is picked up there are no major ups or downs and a reasonable pace can be maintained back to Willsworthy. This is more of an out and back route than many of the other more circular routes but a visit to this impressive rocky valley should be part of any walker's itinerary.

❽ Manaton – Sheer Enjoyment!

Manaton is a small village about five miles from Bovey Tracey on the B3344. The playwright John Galsworthy lived here for many years and wrote *The Forsyte Saga*, amongst other works, at Wingstone, which is only a few hundred yards from the start of this walk. The walk of just under three miles begins from the car park near the church and is just one of many that could be done in this part of Dartmoor as it is particularly well blessed with many miles of signposted foot-paths. In theory you shouldn't get lost but …

Enter the churchyard through the Lych Gate (Lych derives from a German word 'leich' meaning corpse so it was where the coffin was rested before Christian burial). Pass in front of the church and in the shortest of distances you will be confronted with an immediate choice of routes. Turn right and follow a path that seems to have so

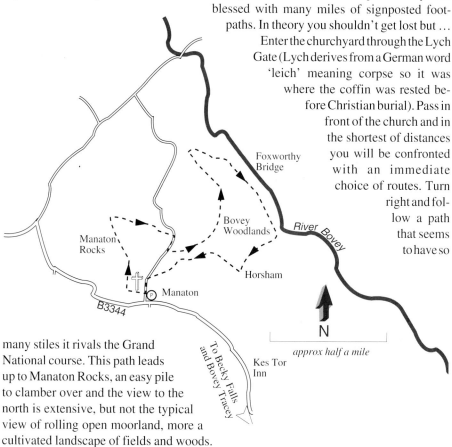

many stiles it rivals the Grand National course. This path leads up to Manaton Rocks, an easy pile to clamber over and the view to the north is extensive, but not the typical view of rolling open moorland, more a cultivated landscape of fields and woods.

Beyond Manaton Rocks the path descends the hill quite sharply and in a short distance it is necessary to bear right on to a much more level path, which leads to a surfaced road. Make sure on this section that you watch out for any embedded stones that stick up those few critical inches above the ground. Our intrepid leader, whilst walking and deliberating over the OS Map at the same time, failed to notice one and was sent sprawling in a most undignified fashion – guaranteed to produce hysterics from the family but it does nothing for the self esteem!

On meeting the road turn right onto it and climb up and over the brow of the hill. In a short distance take the first turn on the left, which is a surfaced road and passes some attractive houses. This ends with a cattle grid or stile, depending on your preference. Here

23

you need to take care to go the right way for the track that crosses the field is not the one you want. If you look closely you may just discern a faint path bisecting the road and the hedge boundary. This you should follow gently downwards to cross a few obstacles, more stiles, before reaching a much clearer and obvious path. Turn left and follow this one through the woods dropping downhill, first gently and then more steeply.

A road is met at what appears to be the bottom of the hill. Turn right and walk along it towards Foxworthy Bridge. After a few hundred yards this road bends and drops more steeply towards the River Bovey. Before you reach the river there is a path, signposted, off to your right, which should be followed. Apart from the occasional muddy patch this is an easy path contouring the valley side of Neaden Cleave. Along this section you may like to play 'Spot the Nesting Boxes'. Whether or not these detached residences for our feathered friends have vacant possession or not will depend upon the season.

Eventually you'll meet a T-junction with a path coming straight down the hill. If you have some surplus energy you can go downhill, turning left at the bottom and within yards you will reach Horsham Steps, a miniature version of Becky Falls, which is a lovely spot for a picnic or rest. If, however, you wish to get back to the car more quickly, you must turn right at the T-junction and climb steeply upwards. Whatever your choice you will have to climb this steep slope sooner or later. It is the hardest climb on the walk and it is always worth pausing to 'enjoy the view' – even if the view is obscured by trees!

Continue with the path, ignoring the one coming down from the right, and on reaching some lovely old cottages turn right and head for 'Manaton' and not 'Water'. The track is

An old view of Manaton Church

a good one and it should not be too long before you see Manaton Church ahead of you. If you are so disposed, and if the Kestor Inn is open, you can take your family off for a well deserved drink half a mile down the road at Water, or for a cream tea at Becky Falls another half mile further on.

❾   A Tour of the Best Tors on the Moor

Haytor on eastern Dartmoor is one of the best known landmarks in Devon. Each year several thousand visitors park their cars beneath the rock and stroll up to its twin granite masses. Over one third of the Devonshire landscape can be seen from this vantage point. Many folk settle for this brief excursion as their day out on Dartmoor and return home unaware of the delights and attractions in the vicinity of this famous old rock. Here is a walk for you to consider in an area of unparalleled beauty, steeped in history and legend.

The lower car park at Haytor provides free parking. The first stage of the walk is not

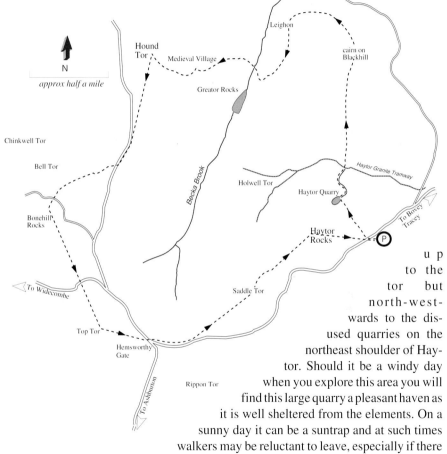

up to the tor but north-west-wards to the disused quarries on the northeast shoulder of Haytor. Should it be a windy day when you explore this area you will find this large quarry a pleasant haven as it is well sheltered from the elements. On a sunny day it can be a suntrap and at such times walkers may be reluctant to leave, especially if there is a biting wind. There is a pond in the quarry, which is far deeper than it appears to be. In it swim huge goldfish – no doubt exiled from a more domestic situation, but now sufficiently hardy to thrive in a location that can be like a cauldron on a hot summer day or a deep freeze in the icy grip of a Dartmoor winter

Leading from the quarry is the first railroad to have been built in Devon. However its main claim to fame is that the lines were made of granite from the quarries as it was cheaper and more accessible than importing metal for the rails. The granite quarrying

enterprise, which began in 1820 with great optimism, faltered in the face of competition from more easily accessible Cornish granites, less than a half a century later. Your route lies, for about one hundred yards, along the branch line leading out of the Haytor quarry to a junction with the main tramway line. Before you head north-eastwards across Haytor Down towards Black Hill, it may be worth examining the 'points', also of granite, which switched the wagons toward their destination.

The beauty of the stroll to Black Hill is that the terrain is so gentle on the feet that the rambler can enjoy the surroundings at every step. Whether your eyes take in the view of distant tankers in the English Channel or prefer to scan the far horizons of Somerset's hills is a matter of preference. However, at the cairn on Black Hill there is only one way to look, and that is down into the valleys of the Becka Brook and Bovey rivers.

Model aeroplane enthusiasts are frequent visitors to this location as their models perform well with the lifting air currents – they need their thermals!

Some skills are now necessary to reach the desired path. The way down from Black Hill is steep and the force of gravity will be all too apparent so it will be necessary to apply the brakes on this next section. A generally northward direction needs to be followed, steeply downhill, for a few hundred yards until a rough track will be met running above fields. On reaching it follow it left or westwards. After a short stretch of gentle gradients it plunges down the hillside towards the steep depression carved by the Becka Brook. The large hill immediately ahead of you is Manaton Rocks, which is featured in another of the walks in this book. By now you will have seen some of the different types of scenery on Eastern Dartmoor. It is an area well served by a complicated network of country lanes and, dare we say it, it is almost impossible to get lost around here! With such famous last words ringing in your ears, skirt the edge of Leighon to stay with the path that runs around the hillside on a southward course. Beyond two fields, which will be on your left hand side, the track will drop down on its way to cross the Becka Brook. If you are going to encounter muddy conditions on this walk, then this next section is the most likely spot. To add insult to injury there is a sharp climb upwards on the other side of the valley but, if you keep in mind that there is some great moor and tor landscape ahead, it is a worthwhile slog.

One natural attraction and one man-made are the rewards on reaching the open moor once more. The tor on your left is the weirdest looking mass of rocks on the moor and is called Greator Rocks. It has several summits and is ideal for clambering over or simply to sit on to survey the surrounding scenery. Ahead lies the Hound Tor Mediaeval Village, excavated in 1961. This settlement was probably abandoned in the fourteenth century, possibly because of the devastating effects of the Black Death, a plague which killed almost half the population of north-west Europe. The village had about a dozen buildings and was a farming community. Corn was grown in the small fields and animals were grazed on the poorer pastures. It must have been a remote existence but several generations of families lived there from the tenth century up to the death of the village four centuries later.

The next destination, Hound Tor, is one of the largest rock piles on Dartmoor and its closeness to a road assures it of public attention with the hordes in evidence on fine days scrambling over the various piles. There are apparent gaps between the various columns of rock, which makes Hound Tor a fine example of what geographers term an 'avenue tor'.

Sometimes it is difficult to give precise directions in a book such as this and when people misinterpret well-intentioned route directions it can invariably lead to them getting lost. Some are philosophical in such a situation whereas others write to the author! The next bit needs to be carefully followed and it calls for a sense of awareness.

Most walkers have an aversion to road walking so to minimise the route pounding on Tarmac for this outing it is necessary to head almost south or slightly west of it across Houndtor Down. If you are not carrying a compass you can work out your course by observing a row of trees that line the road, which leads southwards also. By steering a walking course parallel to them, until the last is reached, and then heading to where a dry stone wall comes down to meet this road, you will cut down the road walking section to just a few hundred yards. Walk along the right side of the road, downhill, and you will learn from a sign on the opposite side that bulls in fields with heifers or cows are not likely to cause walkers any problems. Feeling much better and enlightened from this gem of country lore, cross the cattle grid and you will relocate open moorland.

Turn right and strike out away from the road. You will see, almost immediately, a rockpile on your right, which is Bell Tor. However, this is not your destination and you should head to the left of this impressive tor. This also has the advantage of enabling you to skirt some boggy terrain.

The next landmark is one of the most pleasing-to-the-eye rock piles of the 234 (or so) tors on the moor. Bonehill Rocks also gives an excellent view down the valley of the East Webburn, with the tall tower of St Pancras Church of Widecombe in the Moor a readily identifiable landmark. Top Tor lies just over a half mile to the south-south-east of Bonehill Rocks and is the next point to head for. Although there is a general upward trend in the walking required to reach this tor, the gradient is mild and the going underfoot very accommodating. Walking on moorland like this is far less demanding on calf muscles than on stony tracks or surfaced roads.

Top Tor is appropriately named and gives a more panoramic view than many of the tors visited today. If the weather is clear enough you will be able to see the television mast of North Hessary Tor, on the hill above Princetown, about 10 miles away to the west, as the crow flies.

For the next mile or so the main Widecombe to Haytor road will be in view so the name of the game will be to avoid having to walk on its hard surface, or to dodge its traffic. This is no problem. From Top Tor head down towards Hemsworthy Gate, a junction where the road from Ashburton meets the Widecombe road. Keep an eye open for the ghost of a horseman who rides the road from Haytor towards Hemsworthy (see *Dark and Dastardly Dartmoor*). Also you should not bear too far to the right on a line from Top Tor to Hemsworthy Gate as there is an area of very wet land and it would be such a shame to reach the final section of the walk only to become engulfed in a foul smelling mire! Although it's prone to be wet, it's not a dangerously boggy patch.

From Hemsworthy Gate you will need to stay quite close to, but not necessarily on, the road for a very short while. On your left is Saddle Tor. Once you have climbed over this rocky hill you will see Haytor Rocks. Saddle Tor is so named because when seen from a distance, in tandem with Haytor, the elevated feature resembles a saddle. It is more than likely that you will have climbed sufficient rocks as is necessary to satiate your climbing requirements today. Haytor, like the others, is optional. It is quite an easy assignment to pass by the base of this eminent pile, enjoy its wondrous view over South Devon, and head downhill to your vehicle in the lower car park.

The map says you have done about six miles, but if you have indulged in the energetic exigencies of tor climbing your body will no doubt tell you that you have done more!

The view towards Widecombe from Bonehill Rocks

⑩ Warren House and the Land of Mines

There are two possible starting points for this expedition in an area of former tin mines with such great names as Vitifer and The Golden Dagger Mine. You can park near the famous Warren House Inn, on the B3212, a few miles to the north-east of Postbridge, or you can park in the small car park at Bennett's Cross, less than half a mile along the same road towards Moretonhampstead. Bennet or Bennett's Cross is a rough hewn piece of granite and a minimum amount of masonry effort seems to have gone into it. The 'WB' initials on it are believed to stand for Warren Bounds. A warren is a place where rabbits were kept for breeding, and later eating, and these were the basic diet for the tinners who toiled away in the bowels of the earth all around the district. Their pub was on the opposite side of the road to the inn you see today and its name is another acknowledgement to the importance of rabbits.

But that's enough of the rabbiting on – let's start the walk. If you parked near the Warren House Inn, where

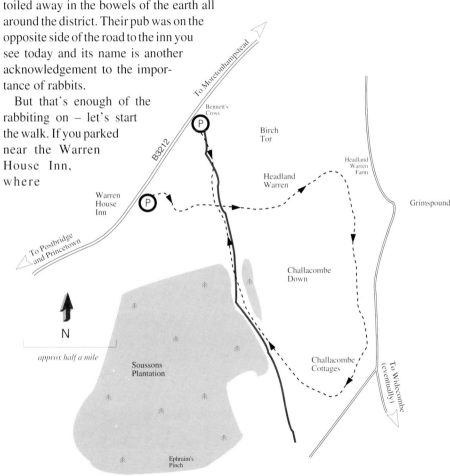

there is a small car park on the left (just before the inn if you are travelling towards Postbridge) you will find a broad track heading straight out of it. For its first few hundred yards you will run parallel with a line of telegraph poles, which will not be too far away at any time in the first mile or so of the walk.

29

To reach the valley bottom, by the most direct route, leave the main track, not far from the lower slopes of the hill, to descend a much steeper and rougher track. This takes you to a point where you can easily cross the small Redwater Brook running down from Bennett's Cross.

If you start from Bennett's Cross you need to make your way southwards for a short distance until you pick up the depression of the Redwater Brook, which will take you down to the same point. Almost until the very end of the walk the route will be identical.

The tin mines, which later also produced iron ore, operated from the early eighteenth century through to about the time of the First World War. As you head eastwards towards Headland Warren you will see the enormous gullies associated with the industry. Long gone are the waterwheels that operated the crushing stamps, the miners' cottages and the

ponies that carted away the products of their efforts. The tin miners were of the toughest breed of men and a pub filled with them, after they had done a hard day's graft, was not a place for the mild-mannered or faint-hearted!

The tracks in this vicinity will spare you the problem of negotiating the gullies, which you would find, should you ever traverse them, a very time-consuming, energy-draining version of a moorland big dipper.

From the valley bottom you will see a path that climbs the hillside, to the right of the poles and to the left of a stone walled enclosure. The hill starts gently but becomes a bit steeper. The path takes us high to a col or pass between Challacombe and Birch Tor.

It will not be long before you reach Headland Warren Farm. Long ago this was the Birch Tor Inn, another meeting place for the hard drinking tinners. It bore a sign on its door that informed any uninitiated customers that "Jan Roberts lives here and sells whisky and beer, your hearts for to cheer; and if you want meat to make up a treat here be rabbits to eat". In the last part of the nineteenth century James Hannaford lived here with his dog. He would walk more or less the same route that you have covered so far on this trek. Unfortunately on one occasion he got too near one of the old shafts and toppled in, only being saved from certain death by some handily placed timbers. His dog sat at the top of the shaft until a search party arrived in the vicinity, then he barked for all he was worth leading them to rescue a grateful, but badly injured, James Hannaford.

Hopefully avoiding any such problems, you descend to this settlement turning right onto a signed bridlepath beside this dwelling. Walk past the stable block and along the surfaced road for the shortest of distances. On your right is a gate with 'footpath' clearly marked on it.

Thus leave Headland Warren and its colourful past behind. There is a most pleasant and level path leading up in a southerly direction. It is quite probable that this section will be the most sheltered along the route as the prevailing wind is a westerly flow and you have the great hill of Challacombe Down to protect you.

Leave the confines of Headland Warren via a gate in a stone wall that looks somewhat out of place. The going is excellent underfoot apart from a narrow piece of boggy ground, which needs to be sidestepped. It provides any gallant walker with an opportunity to be chivalrous and to do a modern day version of a Sir Walter Raleigh or a St Christopher, although it usually ends up as every man for himself.

By more or less staying on the same level you will soon reach a short terrace of three cottages – Challacombe Cottages and farther on another dwelling and outbuildings. Head on past them but steer right and climb up to a gateway with a signpost. The Bennett's Cross direction will serve nicely and in the next few hundred yards you will change direction from south, through west, to north. At the same time it's likely your leeward aspect will be replaced by a windward one and progress may be impeded if the westerly wind is blowing.

A moorland view thus gives way to a forest view as the enormous plantation of Soussons Down will be seen away to the left. Just over half a mile away to the south west and on the southern edge of the forest is a little hill with the strange name of Ephraim's Pinch, where leg-

A buddle complete with all its working parts

end has it that poor Ephraim met an untimely death trying to prove to his would-be father-in-law of his worthiness to marry his daughter (see *Dark and Dastardly Dartmoor*).

The path though is still easy and drops down to an old fashioned form of stile. There is a clump of trees on the right side of your desired track and a forest beyond the stream. In between are many more industrial remains from the mining days of this valley. There are buildings, and a curious circular structure, called a buddle, plus a disused dry leat that lies below the track you follow until you cross the tiny trickle of a stream. Ignore the track signposted to the left.

Proceed on up the west bank of the stream and you will reach the point where you were an hour or so ago. Those bound for Bennett's Cross will carry on straight ahead whilst those heading back to the Warren House and, no doubt a well-earned drink, will need to bear left and climb the hill, once more beside the poles, in a west bound direction to reach their vehicle. This is a stroll of about four miles and the bulk of it has been relatively easy apart from (as we always say) the bits that weren't!

OTHER TITLES FROM OBELISK PUBLICATIONS

DIARY OF A DARTMOOR WALKER
Chips Barber

Diary of a Dartmoor Walker is a light-hearted book which includes many unusual strolls, rambles, excursions, expeditions, safaris, pilgrimages and explorations into all areas of the Dartmoor National Park. There is the Lich Way, or the way of the dead (and the dying!), the Abbot's Way, the North/South Crossing and even the Tom Cobley Walk. This 'diary' spans the four seasons to capture Dartmoor in a way that no other book has managed so far – and the walks are quite interesting too!

DIARY OF A DEVONSHIRE WALKER
Chips Barber

In this amusing and entertaining book, Chips Barber describes his walks over Dartmoor, the Haldon Hills and along the Devonshire coastline in his own inimitable style. We are confident that anyone who reads *Diary of a Devonshire Walker* will want to get onto the boulder-strewn landscape of the open moors or along the rugged South Devon coastline. This is a walking book with a difference, one that no self respecting lover of the Devon countryside should be without.

THE GREAT WALKS OF DARTMOOR
Terry Bound

This book is a 'must' for any serious Dartmoor walker! It features all the classic long walks that Dartmoor offers: the Abbots' Way, the Lich Way, the OATS walk, the Dartmoor Perambulation, the Mariners' Way and the Ten Tors. It is an invaluable guide for anyone who might be considering one of the marathon type Dartmoor walks.

THE GREAT LITTLE DARTMOOR BOOK
Chips Barber

Beautifully illustrated with line drawings on every page, it features stories of the Moor's folklore and legends, walking and 'Letterboxing', villages and towns, wildlife and tors, pubs and entertainment. This small book is the perfect "all in one" guide book to Dartmoor.

DARK AND DASTARDLY DARTMOOR
Sally and Chips Barber

Dartmoor is an ancient landscape steeped in a wealth of folklore, legends and ghost stories, some based on fact, others passed on by word of mouth. Read about the Devil and his hounds, headless horses, pigs in wigs, phantom cottages, and examine the unique "Ghost Map of Dartmoor".

THE A TO Z OF DARTMOOR TORS
Terry Bound

Terry Bound has visited nearly every known and unknown tor on and around the moor and uses his considerable knowledge to identify other landmarks and distinguishing features. With this invaluable guide on their bookshelves, no Dartmoor enthusiast need ever again be in any doubt as to the identity or location of any Tor.

WEIRD AND WONDERFUL DARTMOOR
Sally and Chips Barber

Weird and Wonderful Dartmoor is packed with amusing anecdotes and stories, some stranger than fiction, that could only happen in a place like Dartmoor! Read about many of the bizarre escape bids from Dartmoor Prison, how a rat set a mill alight, about a henpecked husband and a goose-pecked vicar, and Dartmoor's more exotic wildlife — llamas, crocodiles and elephants. You don't believe there are any of these on Dartmoor? Then read this little book and discover just how Weird and Wonderful Dartmoor really is!

TV & FILMS ALL …MADE IN DEVON,
Chips Barber and David FitzGerald

Devon has been used extensively for the making of many films, adverts and television programmes. *Made in Devon* is a comprehensive and entertaining guide to a vast number of film productions made all over the county. Packed with amazing behind-the-scenes stories, it reveals the tricks of how Devon has become the Mediterranean, Tropical Rain Forests, Monte Carlo, Distant Planets, Scotland, West Indian islands, California and many other places. You will be amazed at how many famous and well-known film stars have visited Devon.

BEAUTIFUL DARTMOOR, Chips Barber

Dartmoor is a land often described as England's last great wilderness and there are remote tracts of land where you can wander for miles without seeing another person. In contrast, within Dartmoor's 365 square miles there are popular places where crowds are drawn to savour Dartmoor's unique atmosphere. Chips Barber has compiled over 30 colourful photos to create a lasting souvenir of this magnificent and inspiring landscape.

For further details of these or any of our Devon titles, please contact:
Obelisk Publications, 2 Church Hill, Pinhoe, Exeter EX4 9ER
tel: Exeter 468556.